MINDGLOW

by
Bob Stanish

photographs by Jon Stanish

Cover by Tom Sjoerdsma

Copyright © Good Apple, Inc., 1986

ISBN No. 0-86653-346-X

Printing No. 9876

GOOD APPLE, INC.
BOX 299
CARTHAGE, IL 62321-0299

ACKNOWLEDGEMENTS

With fatherly pride to my son, Jon Stanish, for his photographs.

To a group of lovable, warm, bright and creative kids from the Dickinson Independent School District, Dickinson, Texas:

Elizabeth Ann Bell	Sheri Burmaster	Vikki Johnson
Ines Betancourt	Hai Huynh	Bonnie Trahan
Anjanette Burns	Kris Luke	Michael Devall
Emily Clock	Barbara Murray	Charlene Downey
Alison Curtis	Danielle Abshire	Audrey Ferguson
Bryce Denney	Ivonne Acosta	Kirk Harstad
Brandy Donivan	Vanessa Alexander	Natalie Thompson
Allison Frazar	Teri Allen	Robert Heflin
Micah Heimlich	Bonabeth Bell	Kris Jones
David Hanson	Duke Brudner	Michael Kulvicki
Kitt Hirasaki	David Doyle	Derek McBride
Chad Martin	Mathew Doyle	Katrina Seale
Jeffrey McCollum	Ann Finney	Anita Tipps
David Morales	Allison Gullion	Ryan Walter
John Payne	Misty Kyle	Autumn White
Sergio Renovato	E.J. Manheimer	Kellye Bolton
Ginny Reynolds	Brian Moore	Chris Childress
Don Sides	Aaron Rader	Sean Lewis
Randall Smith	James Shinn	Mathew St. John
Tim Wilder	Robert Cernosek	Mary Timmons
Brent Wolfort	Nancy Blasberg	Richard Bennett
Jeremy Eubanks	Jaimie Garrett	Jennifer Groves

for being a group of receptive receivers for *Mindglow*.

And,

To a group of professionals who read the manuscript and offered some suggestions that improved what I had:

Barbara Dixon, educational consultant, Orangeville, Ontario
Patricia Doyle, teacher of the gifted, Williamsville, New York
Bob Eberle, author and consultant, Edwardsville, Illinois
Audrey Lederman, author and teacher, Miami, Florida
Carol Wittig, gifted programming specialist and graduate student in Creative Studies at State University College at Buffalo

TABLE OF CONTENTS

NTRODUCTION

WHY DID I WRITE MINDGLOW?

I went through a period in my life in which things no longer glowed. The positive elements I used to see became out of focus. In my search for self, and it is still continuing, I learned and relearned a number of things. For two and a half years I wrote and established statements—statements to believe in, statements to live by—a philosophy for me.

MINDGLOW evolved around the statements. It is not my intent to cause my statements to be universal for anyone. They are, however, a MINDGLOW for me.

HOW TO MINDGLOW . . .

1. FIRST, think of an environment that is special to you—an environment that will cause you to blend thought with feeling. Some of my environments are the early morning hours, warm fireplaces and the patterns and textures of a wooded retreat. Find an environment that will work for you.

Take **Mindglow** and slowly read the statements found in "mind glitter" and "more mind glitter." Look at the photographs as they appear and take time for your own experiences and thoughts to evolve.

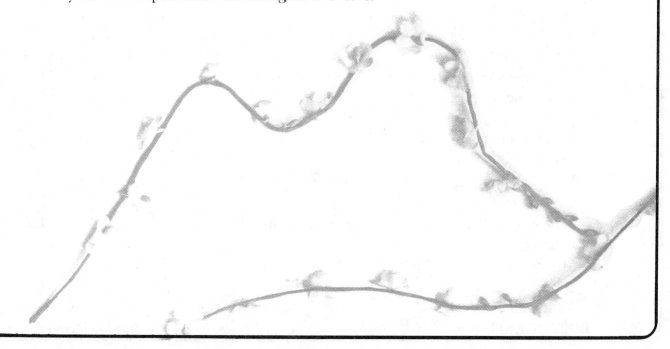

2 SECOND, leaf through **Mindglow** until a particular activity catches your eye. Read it and think about the processes of thinking that are required. Visualize the "Structure of the Intellect Model" of J.P. Guilford and the dimensions of **contents**, **products**, and **operations**. There was a purposeful intent to interplay all of the elements of **contents** with the **products** of **transformations** and **implications**. This was done through an emphasis on **convergent**, **divergent**, and **evaluative operations**. The reason for this is to promote those factors that contribute to expanding creative thought. There are opportunities within each activity to involve E. Paul Torrance's factors of creative thinking (**fluency**, **flexibility**, **elaboration**, and **originality**) in our daily lives. And finally, components of **Creative Problem-Solving** are here, too. Not in the step-by-step process that is so familiar to so many. But it's there because it is integrated with whatever I do.

3 THIRD, once you have internalized the thoughts, the feelings, the processes of **Mindglow**, **insert**, **modify** or **force-fit** the activities into whatever you are teaching. Do not use the activities as fillers for a substitute teacher. There is too much of a risk. It takes a MINDGLOW state of mind to teach MINDGLOW.

4 FOURTH, take what you can from **Mindglow** into your own personal life. There is a quantity of things here, things to consider. Do not rush through the book. Just allow time for the connections and the extensions to be made.

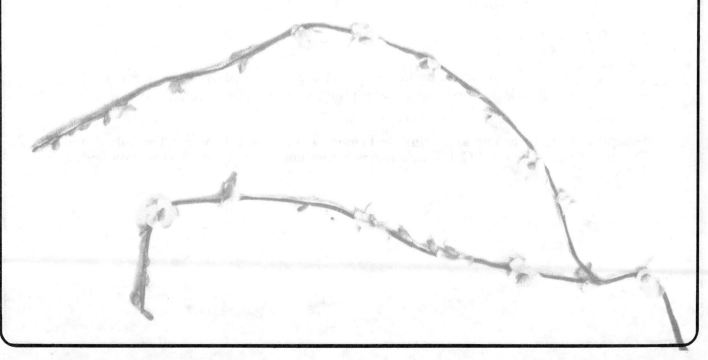

WHAT'S IN A MINDGLOW ACTIVITY?

• MIND GLITTER AND MORE MIND GLITTER . . .

These are statements of a philosophical nature, a base or foundation from which an exercise was created.

• FOCUS[1] . . .

These are the qualities of effective teaching. Each activity exercise will focus on several of these indicators.

These are:

QUESTIONING TECHNIQUES

Promoting the ability to ask questions that stimulate, expand, and extend knowledge. Questioning that effects metaphorical thought and insight, inquiry and open-endedness.

CREATIVE INVENTIVENESS

Promoting the ability to reverse some accepted notions. Encouraging invention, construction and supposing. Coming up with different ways of doing things. Causing one to visualize what's behind and beyond closed doors.

SELF-DIRECTED ACTIVITY

Promoting the ability to go beyond the expected, the given, or the assigned, and the freedom, flexibility and the encouragement to do so.

OPENNESS

Promoting a desire to respect and to accept unusual or provocative ideas. Encouraging, accepting, and responding to challenges.

[1]Adapted from an article appearing in **Tempo** (Texas Association for the Gifted and Talented). Vol. V, No. 3. "G/T Teachers Are Something Special," by Bob Stanish Spring 1985.

HUMOR

The ability to laugh and effect a sense of humor. Utilizing humor as a means of cultivating originality in thought. The ability to laugh at oneself.

KNOWLEDGE

The ability to acquire and respond to information. The ability to utilize a wide variety of processes to receive information. The ability to put information to use in traditional and innovative ways. The ability to gather more information from provided information.

THINKING TIME

The ability to make time for the playing around, experimenting, and the examination of ideas and concepts.

RESOURCES

The ability to find and/or create resources that stimulate curiosity, discovery, and enlightenment. Putting resources to use in both traditional and creative ways.

INTEGRATION

The ability to synthesize. The ability to think about universal issues. The ability to find and make associations and see relationships.

ASSESSMENT

The ability to assess outcomes and products. The ability to develop criteria to evaluate solutions.

INTERPERSONAL REGARD

The ability to commend, to accept, to help, to promote the dignity and individuality of others.

- **PROCEDURES . . .**

    Suggestions on how to approach the exercise.

- **EXTENSIONS . . .**

    Suggestions on how to extend the exercise into other realms or simply just another way of approaching the concept or the process.

ALSO, THROUGHOUT THE BOOK THERE IS . . .

CREATING A MINDGLOW CLIMATE FOR ALL SEASONS. . .

    Beginning on page 14 and continuing on page 18 are some suggestions for establishing a classroom climate. To be sure, the suggestions reflect my values and beliefs and experiences.

REMEMBRANCES . . .

    These are ancedotes of some past experiences that have some association to the present. REMEMBRANCES can be found on pages 46, 60, 70, and 76.

THE ARTWORK

Sometimes I take my classes into a field to find things. We look for things that please us. They might be of a unique design or shape or texture. They might be something found within something—just things found in a field and something special.

I take what they find and place them, one at a time, on a photographic copy machine. I give each child a copy of what he found. He writes a poem or a thought or a memory on that page. What the children write must have an association with what they found. The association may be symbolic or figural or semantic with its title.

It seemed to me this would be appropriate for this book. The artist is nature. We present to you what we found and enjoyed and became special in our lives and minds.

Bob Stanish

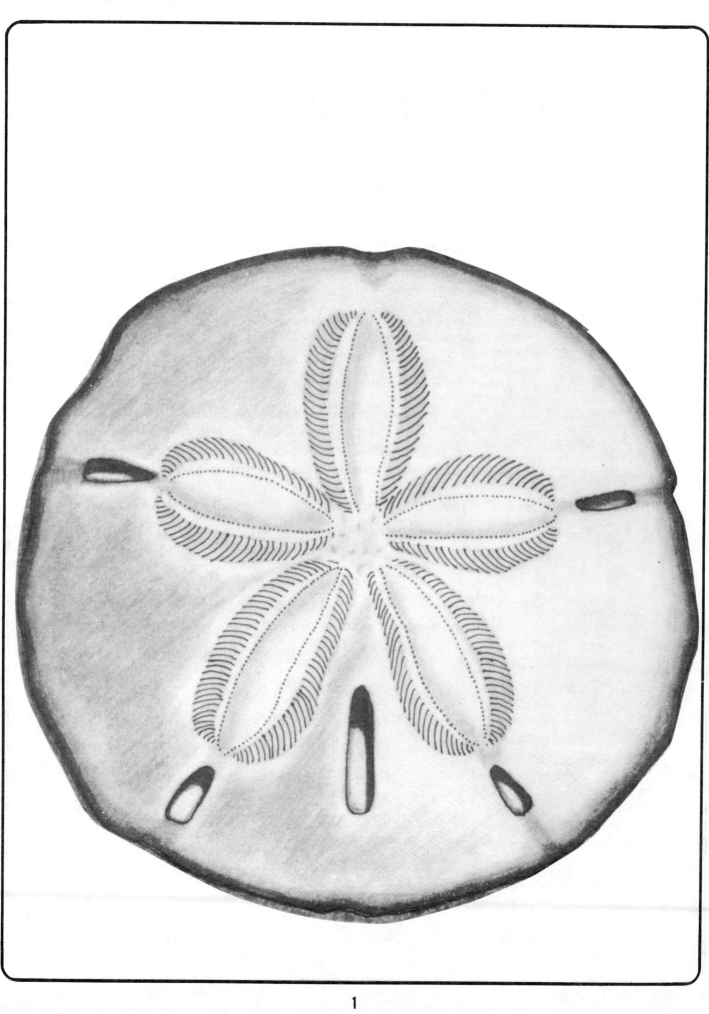

SAND DOLLARS

Focus: Questioning Techniques
Creative Inventiveness

MIND GLITTER

There is structure within all things—sand dollars, spiderwebs, snowflakes and even the wind, for it blows in its current. Creative thinking requires structure too, if it is to flow.

The structure for creative thought is the way the question is structured or the problem stated. Sometimes a format is good because it can extend the mind to diverge further into realms of new understandings.

PROCEDURES:

Present this question to your students: **In what ways might a sand dollar design be used in creating original or different products?**

Before beginning the brainstorming session, select a few student recorders to record student responses. Begin the session by holding up or displaying the illustration of the sand dollar.

During the session, interject with your voice every 30 seconds or so several of the suggested questions on the next page.

1. What could you create by imagining the design is large, then very large?

2. What could you create by imagining the design has texture?

3. What could you create by imagining you could remove a portion of the design?

4. What could you create by imagining the design could float?

5. What could you create by imagining the design is small, then microsmall?

6. What could you create by imagining the design has taste?

7. What could you create by imagining the design is sticky or adhesive?

8. What could you create by imagining the design is ornamental?

9. What could you create by imagining the design could fly?

10. What could you create by imagining the design could be inflated or filled with something?

11. What could you create by imagining the design could be suspended from something?

12. What could you create by imagining the design has an odor?

13. What could you create by imagining the design could be entered?

14. What could you create by imagining the design is transparent?

15. What could you create by imagining the design could be squeezed?

16. What could you create by imagining the design could cover things?

17. What could you create by imagining the design could be played on, stood on, or has the strength to resist pressure or stress?

18. What could you create by imagining the design is at an angle or standing on the rim of its structure?

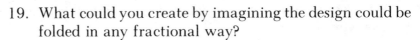

19. What could you create by imagining the design could be folded in any fractional way?

20. What could you create by imagining the design is sagging in the center or in some other location?

21. What could you create by imagining the design is a system or a network?

22. What could you create by imagining the design to be a world within a world?

23. What could you create by imagining the design as a design?

24. What could you create by imagining the design as a cover or a container?

25. What could you create by imagining the design as something washable?

26. What could you create by imagining the design as a component to something else?

27. What could you create by imagining the design could emit sound?

28. What could you create by imagining the design in movement or motion?

29. What could you create by imagining the design as a structure?

30. What could you create by imagining the design joined with more of its kind in varying arrangements or positions?

31. What could you create by imagining the design as a twistable?

32. What could you create by imagining the design as something cozy or comfortable?

33. What could you create by imagining the design as a disposable?

34. What could you create by imagining the design to be adaptable to heat or cold or wetness?

35. What could you create by imagining the design to be whatever you wanted it to be?

EXTENSIONS:

1. Encourage students to develop a criteria to determine what design functions are possible in regard to cost, practicality, attractiveness, uniqueness, etc. Use these factors in selecting the best ideas brainstormed.

2. Try this approach with a selected geometric design—with a design selected from nature like a leaf, a spiderweb, a walnut, etc.

3. Research the attributes of a sand dollar; then think of ways of improving it.

4. Research the symbolic meaning of the sand dollar.

5. Speculate on why the sand dollar is called a sand dollar. Why not call it a sand peso, a sand lire, a sand franc, a sand yen? Encourage self-directed study into the reasons why.

6. Do drawn diagrams of what you think the inner structure of a sand dollar is like; then investigate the reality of that structure.

7. Ask questions like . . .
   "In what ways is a subway like a sand dollar?"
   "In what ways am I like a sand dollar?"
   "In what ways is the universe like a sand dollar?"

8. **SAND DOLLARS** can be associated with the step of "Idea-Finding" in Creative Problem-Solving. For a brief overview, the six steps of Creative Problem-Solving are listed on the following page.

*Step I. **Mess-Finding**: A search for challenges and concerns based on experiences and associations. Once the challenge or concern is accepted, then an effort is made to respond to it.

Step II. **Data-Finding**: Information, impressions, perceptions, and feelings are gathered and examined from varying frames of references. The most important data is selected and analyzed.

Step III. **Problem-Finding**: Possible problem and sub-problem statements are cited. The most important statement is selected.

Step IV. **Idea-Finding**: The use of creative and critical thinking to address the problem statement. Ideas that seem the most promising are selected.

Step V. **Solution-Finding**: The generation of criteria to evaluate the most promising ideas are made. The most important criteria items are selected.

Step VI. **Acceptance-Finding**: A plan of action for implementing the most promising solutions is made. Sources of assistance and resistance have been considered and implemented into the plan. Action is initiated.

*Adapted from **Creative Problem-Solving: The Basic Course** (Isaksen and Treffinger, 1985).

IN WHAT WAYS WOULD LIFE BE DIFFERENT IF . . . ?

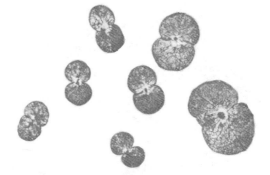

Focus: Questioning Techniques
            Openness
            Knowledge
            Assessment

MIND GLITTER   *Having students respond to paradoxes quickly will fine-tune their abilities to analyze the problems of tomorrow. If there are any benefits from teaching, the greatest one by far is causing someone to think.*

PROCEDURES: Use these questions sparingly—like when there is time in between classes or that time before dismissal.

1. In what ways would life be different if nothing fossilized?
2. In what ways would life be different if we had no moon?
3. In what ways would life be different if mold or fungus did not appear?
4. In what ways would life be different if ice didn't form?
5. In what ways would life be different if sleep wasn't necessary?
6. In what ways would life be different if taste was eliminated?
7. In what ways would life be different if there were no mountains?
8. In what ways would life be different if nothing could float?
9. In what ways would life be different if there were no shadows?
10. In what ways would life be different if there were no insects?
11. In what ways would life be different if continents were all connected?
12. In what ways would life be different if life expectancy was 200 years?
13. In what ways would life be different if memories were only retained for a year?

14. In what ways would life be different if feelings were not felt?

15. In what ways would life be different if a growing season was a full year?

16. In what ways would life be different if there were no salt in the ocean?

17. In what ways would life be different if the force of gravity was reduced in half?

18. In what ways would life be different if change did not occur?

19. In what ways would life be different if we could visualize tomorrow today?

20. In what ways would life be different if mistakes were not committed?

21. In what ways would life be different if we couldn't dream?

22. In what ways would life be different if dogs didn't bark?

23. In what ways would life be different if we all looked the same?

24. In what ways would life be different if everyone knew his talents?

25. In what ways would life be different if fantasy was gone?

EXTENSION:　　　　　　　　Encourage students to share questions of their own creation.

Note:　　　　With any question, probe for deeper answers. For instance, in question 1, responses should eventually reach the stage of resources and fuels, survival and various fields, if not all, of science.

**MORE
MIND GLITTER**　　　　　　*I like to think that the greatest ideas started with the question, "In what ways would life be different if . . . ?" To improve anything is to make something different. That includes us, too.*

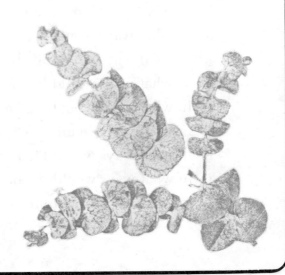

GRAPHICALLY US!

Focus: Interpersonal Regard

Assessment

Openness

MIND GLITTER   *There's a strong difference between classroom manage-*
ment and classroom leadership.

Leadership has something to do with getting others to
manage themselves.

> *People don't want to be managed.*
> *I don't want to be managed.*
> *I want to manage myself.*
> *If I do that well enough maybe . . .*
> *I can lead.*
> *If I can lead,*
> *I can teach.*

PROCEDURES: Encourage students to create pie graphs with percentage
breakdowns on some of the provided topics.

1.   What's important in my life
2.   The attributes of someone I admire in this class
3.   The character traits I admire most of a famous person
4.   How I'd rate this story character in terms of traits
5.   The talents that I have

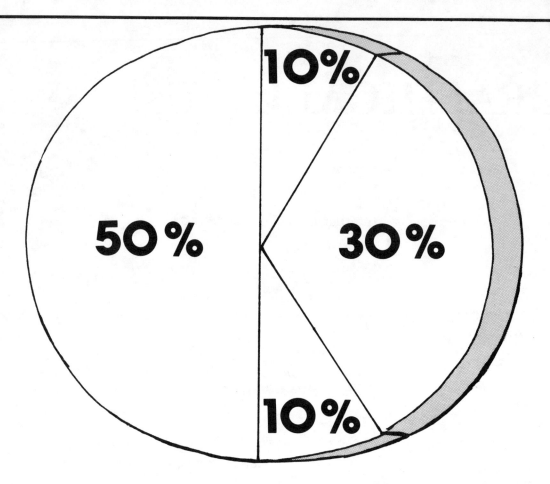

What's important in my life: 50% = thinking
10% = cloud watching
30% = dreaming
10% = miscellaneous

6. The talents that _____ has
7. The most important talents to have
8. How I'd like to organize this class in terms of time
9. How I spend a typical school day in relationship to time
10. How I spend my time and how I'd like to spend my time
11. How I will spend my time in researching this topic
12. How I spend my time on weekends
13. The stuff I eat

EXTENSIONS:

1. If computers and graphic software is available, encourage students to use them in graphing their topics.
2. Use this activity format in teaching percentages and graphs.

LISTING REVISITED

Focus: Questioning Techniques

Knowledge

Thinking Time

Integration

MIND GLITTER

*My favorite activity in **Sunflowering** (Stanish, 1977) has always been "Listing." It is a favorite because it can go from a simple recollection to deep levels of insight and association.*

Taking the time for reflection and thought is so important—observing, perceiving, discovering . . . Contained on the next few pages is another "listing" affecting the effect of recollection.

PROCEDURES:

Use this activity as something to be read to a total group with long pauses between items—just things to reflect on and to consider. Also, it can be used as a brainstorming vehicle for smaller groups or use it yourself in moments of your own privacy.

1. List things that glow.
2. List things to believe.
3. List silent things.
4. List things easy to forget.
5. List things that are wobbly.
6. List things that have no weight.
7. List things that glitter.
8. List large things that are small.
9. List little things that are big.

10. List things that can be reversed.

11. List things that can hurt.

12. List things that cause warmth.

13. List things that stretch.

14. List things that squeak.

15. List things that don't change color.

16. List unbreakable things.

17. List heavy things that have no weight.

18. List silent things that are loud.

19. List spongy things.

20. List infinite things.

21. List the unmovable things.

22. List things that become smaller.

23. List things that fade.

24. List difficult things to share.

25. List things you wouldn't want to lose.

26. List the sounds of twilight.

27. List look-alikes that are not alike.

28. List things without color.

29. List ways to grow.

EXTENSIONS:

1. If brainstorming a selected item, count the number of different categories of thought. For example, in item 9 responses might include a mountain, a promise, an idea, a worry, the Empire State Building, etc.

2. Encourage students to develop their own LISTING activity.

CREATING A MINDGLOW CLIMATE FOR ALL SEASONS . . .

1. After asking a question, allow time for students to think. Refrain from asking another question for at least eight seconds or more. We cannot expect children to think as fast as some of us talk.

2. Build weekly "community meetings" into your schedule with your class. Build a feeling of "community" among all. Push aside desks and chairs and form a circle of openness and warmth.

3. Provide a few minutes at the end of a school day for class responses to open-ended statements like, "today I learned . . . , today I relearned . . . , today I felt best about . . . ."

4. Reduce teacher questioning that begins with "why?" Replace those reductions with questions that begin with "in what ways might we . . . ?"

5. Build a "one-room schoolhouse type of atmosphere" by having students helping students. Promote interpersonal regard.

6. Begin a school day in your classroom with a few minutes of silent thinking. Allow time for those who wish to share thoughts to do so.

7. Promote creative thinking with some structure. Don't say, "Create a better mousetrap!" Do say, "With a clothes hanger, a wood board, a rubber band and another item of your choice, build a better mousetrap!"

8. Encourage students to seek out smaller components of the larger theme. Everything is a part of something larger. Teaching students the art of categorization is an effective way of achieving this.

9. Create lists with your students! List favorite things, list favorite books, list things of beauty, list special challenges, list things that are important, etc.

(continued on page 18)

THE ARMADILLO SHELL

Focus: Questioning Techniques
Creative Inventiveness

MIND GLITTER   *Finding new and better ways of doing things deals with ideas. Ideas are our greatest achievement and they will always be. Causing new ideas to occur among children can be done effectively with curiosity, flexible thinking (switching categories of thought references) and problem solving.*

PROCEDURES: Present this problem to your students: How many different uses for an empty armadillo shell?

After a few minutes of brainstorming, stop the session and tell students you have a way of increasing their thought production. Then proceed to read slowly the following items. Encourage students to write whatever comes to mind on paper. Afterwards total the different responses.

Afterwards, discuss with students the importance of looking at things in different ways when finding solutions to problems.

1.   How many different uses if the shell was suspended?
2.   How many different uses if the shell contained things
  . . . in a living or family room?
  . . . in a kitchen?
  . . . in a bedroom?
  . . . in a bathroom?

. . . in a dining room?

. . . in a utility room, basement, or garage?

. . . in a closet?

3. How many different uses if the shell was on a wall?

4. How many different uses if the shell was on a floor?

5. How many different uses if the shell was on a desk?

6. How many different uses if the shell was on a tree?

7. How many different uses if the shell was on a window-sill?

8. How many different uses if the shell was in a car?

9. How many different uses if the shell was on a patio?

10. How many different uses if the shell was combined with something else?

11. How many different uses if the shell was divided or cut apart in different ways?

12. How many different uses if the shell was placed at different angles or viewed from different positions?

13. How many different uses if the shell

. . . became larger?

. . . became smaller?

. . . became twisted?

. . . had a taste?

. . . had a smell?

. . . had adhesiveness?

. . . changed colors?

. . . was made from different substances or materials?

. . . could be worn?

. . . had something inside to see?

. . . had something inside to hear?

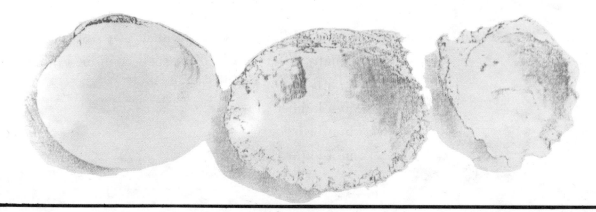

       . . . floated?

       . . . could be squeezed?

       . . . replaced something else?

       . . . hung from a chain or string?

       . . . had a handle?

       . . . had wheels?

       . . . had a hook?

       . . . had four legs?

       . . . had an electric current?

EXTENSIONS:

This activity is teacher-directed brainstorming. Not all brainstorming sessions need to be directed as this one. But it does cause students to view things from different angles, perspectives and frames of references. There will be carryover, if structure of this type is used periodically, to other brainstorming sessions.

1.   Try **Scamper** (Eberle, 1971), as a teacher-directed way of getting students to explore other possibilities during a brainstorming session.

2.   In utilizing this approach, try making available to students crayons and newsprint for generating ideas through imagery.

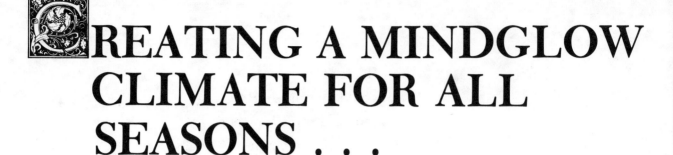

CREATING A MINDGLOW CLIMATE FOR ALL SEASONS . . .

10. Challenge students to discover the world around them. Hundreds of things can be learned from a simple magnifying glass, a school yard with grass, and a library. Discovery is important to learning. Learning is important to discovery. One door can open many doors.

11. Get students to view setbacks, adversity, and failure as important attributes for goal setting and success. The legacy of this can be found in any school library. Challenge students to find the individual stories that are there.

12. The vast majority of all educational resources and materials deal with convergent thinking and memory. Encourage divergent ways of thinking. It really requires both for the skills of living.

13. Separate classroom leadership from classroom management. Concentrate on getting students to manage themselves. That's leadership! Begin by establishing classroom rules with your class.

14. Knowledge grows more effectively and is employed more meaningfully when combined with human sensitivity. As a teacher, affirm your feelings. Affirm who you are!

15. Receive student responses with openness and acceptance.

16. Build up alternatives to a given assignment. There are many different ways to give a book report, many different ways to approach a writing topic and many different ways to present learned information. In doing this you accommodate talents. Talents are avenues by which information can be learned.

17. All disruptive behavior in a classroom is directly related to the interaction of those in that classroom. There are two obvious ways of dealing with disruptive behavior. One is to get rid of interaction. The other way is to improve interaction.

18. Hug the kids you teach! There is nothing wrong with genuine, open affection.

*AMBIGUITIES

Focus: Questioning Techniques   Humor
             Self-Directed Activity   Knowledge
             Thinking Time

MIND GLITTER   *Ambiguities can cause a broad range of thinking skills to occur. One of the factors we need to concern ourselves with is how do we teach kids to solve problems of tomorrow? One way is to fine-tune the processes of problem solving.*

PROCEDURES: Place students in small groups and provide one of these challenges:

1. Describe the size of a rainbow.
2. Write something senseless that makes sense. Explain how the senseless statement makes sense.
3. Rewrite a famous nursery rhyme without using the letters **t** and **h**.
4. Explain the emotion of love without using adjectives or adverbs.
5. Design a gameboard in which there are no losers.
6. Describe how you could explain the workings of a computer to a first grader.
7. Plan a meal without using food items found in a grocery store or someone's garden or farm.
8. Create a dance that explains multiplication.
9. Redesign the human face in order to prevent tooth decay.
10. Determine a useful (beneficial to society) function for cockroaches.
11. Explain justice in less than four sentences.

12. Explain the workings of a Ouija board.

13. Explain the game of football through hand gestures.

14. Describe the properties of weight without using any standard of measurement.

15. Create a word that would be a more effective synonym for the word **ambiguity** than any available.

EXTENSION: List the ambiguities in life, e.g., what would be a more effective road sign for "Dead End"? What would be a more useful way of describing what a toadstool is? In other words, are "ends" really "dead"? Do toads actually sit on stools?

* Ambiguity, as defined in this activity, refers to a lack of clarity or something that doesn't make sense. It can be associated with the "mess" of a poorly defined problem. In other words, we know there's a problem area, but we are not sure what the problem is.

Many times we can gain fresh insights by looking at ambiguities. For instance item 1, "Describe the size of a rainbow," is impossible in terms of standard measurements. However, in terms of measuring spontaneous feelings it may be of great size. So, perhaps one insight into this ambiguity is to take time to account for our feelings in viewing situations, challenges and problems.

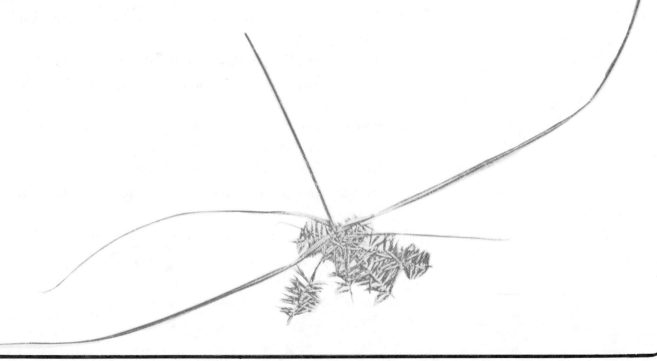

STRUCTURAL INDEXING

Focus:
Knowledge
Thinking Time
Resources
Integration
Assessment

MIND GLITTER

Within all things there is structure. We may not be able to perceive most of it, but it is there. Knowledge has structure too, and, I think, one of the problems we have in schools is teaching content for the sake of content. One of the major issues in American education has always been what to teach. The bodies of information in all academic areas is indeed massive. We need to put content in some order so that student understandings and applications can be made.

I was and still am enchanted by Guilford's Structure of the Intellect, but I was more enchanted with the process he used in formulating the graphic cubic structure itself. So, one day I had the opportunity to ask him and I did. What he did was to lay out index cards on a floor. He did so to see the associations, the connections and the holistic network of it. Index cards are a beautiful instrument to use in whatever work you do. I have used them in demonstrating the principle of Bernoulli, in providing a format for curriculum construction, and for expanding my own thought processes.

PROCEDURES:

Take some index cards and write a major concept or idea on each card—an idea found within a body of an academic discipline. Try the index section of a book for some examples. Lay the cards out to form a grid. Try doing this with nine cards. Study the **random** arrangement you made and create true statements (generalizations) from the words provided. Do this with the words appearing horizontally, vertically and diagonally.

As an example, look at the grid below representing concepts drawn from political science.

politics	resources	culture
change	process	structure
leadership	society	system

Taking the concepts that appear horizontally, these generalizations can be made:

> **Politics** can affect the **resources** within a **culture**.
>
> **Change** a **process** and a **structure** may be changed.
>
> **Leadership** in a **society** can create or destroy a **system**.

Taking the concepts that appear vertically, these generalizations can be made:

> **Politics** can create **change** in **leadership**.
>
> **Resources** can create a **process** for the development of a **society**.
>
> **Culture** determines the **structure** of a **system**.

Taking the concepts that appear diagonally, these generalizations can be made:

> **Politics** can create a **process** for governing a **system**.
>
> **Culture** can create a **process** for developing **leadership**.

EXTENSIONS:

1. Use STRUCTURAL INDEXING as a launching pad for developing generalizations for curriculum development.

2. Use the process for finding out more about yourself. List personal traits and attributes and formalize statements for analysis.

3. Use STRUCTURAL INDEXING as a means of assessing student understandings of a unit of instruction. Actually give students index cards with written concepts, paper and pencil.

4. Use the process as a means of identifying subproblems within a particular problem.

5. Take some personality factors like:

   critical, reserved, concrete thinker, abstract thinker, outgoing, emotionally stable, emotionally less stable, deliberate, impatient, obedient, independent, serious, impulsive, relaxed, tense, controlled, self-conflict, group dependent, self-sufficient, apprehensive, self-assured, tough-minded, tender-minded, expedient, conscientious, etc.

   Place some random-chosen factors on nine index cards in rows of 3's. Some of them, when viewed from a horizontal, vertical, or in a diagonal pattern, will be in conflict. Keeping this in mind, list life situations in which your actions were affected by all three behaviors. We are at times a subtotal of opposites. Hopefully, this will provide us with tolerance—tolerance for ourselves and for others. Even within opposites there is structure!

EXCURSIONS

Focus: Creative Inventiveness   Thinking Time
         Self-Directed Activity   Integration

MIND GLITTER

The mind can wander into voyages of fantastic wonderment. Sometimes, if we allow it, the voyage can bring back a payload of usable information—things that may enrich our lives, solve problems and increase our creative potential.

PROCEDURES:

Try having your students think of ways of improving something. As an example, **in what ways could one improve a doll**, ways in which a child could nurture loving and caring and responsibility?

After a few minutes of brainstorming, stop the session and say: "Close your eyes and imagine you could fly. Imagine how it would feel to fly high in the sky and into and above the clouds. Feel the air currents glide you and feel the warmth of the sun." Allow students time to imagine this voyage and the experiences they encounter.

Stop the fantasy and have them think of words they encountered while they were on this voyage. For instance, maybe the word **warming** or **warm** was encountered. Maybe the concept of a hot-water bottle could improve the doll. A doll with a body temperature could make it more cuddly and loveable.

EXTENSION:

Try this approach in brainstorming possible solutions to a problem or as a way of improving something.

Imagine you have four pieces of earthen pottery to place on a shelf. Each piece of pottery is unique. Each has silhouette of form and beauty.

You experiment with placement. You try placing the tallest pieces on the inside, then the outside. You try alternating the taller pieces with the smaller ones. You try different approaches to gain a perspective of vision.

There are two ways of viewing the pottery placement. One way is through the concept of positive space. In this instance, you make judgements on how the pieces appear next to each other—and how all four pieces appear as a whole.

The other way is seldom used, and it deals with the concept of negative space. There is a silhouette of space between the pieces of pottery. You can arrange the placement of pottery through the perspective of negative space.

Spatial Mnemonics. *There comes a time when we want to remember the shape or form of something. It could be a particular design—free form or geometric. I have a particular way of doing this, and it is what I call spatial mnemonics. It deals with viewing something from two different perspectives, the perspectives of positive and negative space. It goes like this: In my mind, I color the objects of positive space black. I see the silhouette of the design. The next step is to color the objects or the design white in my mind. By doing this, the negative space becomes black. I study the negative space and its particular design in black. The negative space becomes a silhouette. If at some later date, in my mind, I can jigsaw the two then I have correctly recalled the design, the form, the shape of the object or objects.*

Spatial mnemonics have a place in a classroom. It's a strategy that can help kids. It can help kids remember particular forms and shapes. It can have wide application in remembering geographical, political boundaries and geometric shapes; and it has many, many other uses, too. Perhaps the greatest use is that it causes one to examine things from different perspectives.

IMPROVISATION

Focus: Creative Inventiveness
Integration
Thinking Time

MIND GLITTER   *Take a theme and a jazz musician may improvise an embellishment of beauty. It can be done by looking for the combinations, by looking for the components that can create a whole. There is a holistic pattern to everything.*

PROCEDURES: This is a simple pattern found over and over again in nature. It could be a flower, a butterfly, a pansy face, a grouping of pods, a grouping of leaves and so many other things.

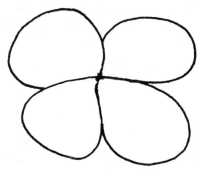

Encourage students to take the design and embellish it so that it functions in a different way. Stimulate thought by asking:

How might it function in a kitchen?
How might it function in a backyard?
How might it function on a beach?
How might it function on an automobile?
How might it function in a library?
How might it function on a mountaintop?
etc.

EXTENSIONS:

1. Display an unshelled walnut and tell students that this design is similar to the human brain. It is also similar to an apple half. How many different things are shaped like the human brain? How many things are shaped like the human heart?

2. Take a design from a snowflake or a seashell or a wasp's nest and do a futuristic design. Describe how this design might function in the year 3000. In what ways might this design be utilized in a city, on the ocean floor or in space?

**MORE
MIND GLITTER**

On another component from the whole:

Our history and our lives have been charted by the teachings of Jesus Christ, Socrates, Gautama Buddha, Mohammed, Confucius, Lao-tse, Mahatma Gandhi and Moses. And within the nations of the Cherokee and the Watusi and within the nations of all cultures, past and present, there have been movers of minds and monolithic structures. These movers became or were chosen to be teachers. Some paid the ultimate price for doing so. Rejoice and be proud to be a teacher.

SENSORING IN

Focus: Thinking Time
Integration

MIND GLITTER

In a field, snowy egrets waited for a December sun to chase away the fog. I've seen fog and morning suns at different times and in different places—sometimes from a frozen cornfield and sometimes from a mountain and sometimes, like today, from the Gulf of Mexico.

Sensory images stored will filter through our consciousnesses in unexpected moments and in unexpected ways. These impulses can be played in a variety of ways towards our own creative development.

PROCEDURES: Provide these three columns to your students:

1. The calm stillness	1. of a meadow	1. is like a memory
2. The effect	2. of a warming sun	2. is like a promise
3. The afterthought	3. of a shimmering pond	3. is like a whisper
4. The image	4. of autumn	4. is like a keepsake
5. The recollection	5. of lengthening shadows	5. is like a friend
6. The anticipation	6. of a winter's chill	6. is like a song
7. The loneliness	7. of a rising tide	7. is like a fading dream
8. The serenity	8. of a waning moon	8. is like me
9. The beauty	9. of a morning's mist	9. is like a book
10. The softness	10. of a rainbow	10. is like a dream

Encourage students to create a combination of three phrases from the three columns. Example: The image of a winter's chill is like a fading dream (4-6-7).

EXTENSIONS:

1. Construct a paragraph around the sentence combination chosen; then construct a story around that paragraph.

2. As a class, create three different columns of sensory images and use them in the same way as described.

3. Create music to fit a sentence.

4. Describe how a certain sentence actually fits a personal experience.

5. Look for similar phrasing from well-known authors.

6. Use the three-column approach with the development of character sketches for the purpose of writing fictional stories.

Example:

Characters	Personality Attributes	Roles
Ginny	silent	friend
Bryce	forceful	leader
Kitt	thoughtful	companion
Allison	dependable	partner
etc.	etc.	etc.

Combinations: Ginny is a silent friend.
Ginny is a thoughtful but forceful partner.
Ginny is a silent, dependable and thoughtful companion.

In using this approach, brainstorm numerous character names, personality attributes, and roles. Allow students to play with combinations and imagine the characters developing in their minds. Allow time for doing this in silence.

Try this approach with historical personalities. Be sure to brainstorm first.

Try this approach before assigning a story to be read. Then, as a class, develop sentences that would describe the characters in the story.

Try this approach in a study on leadership.

Try this approach independently by asking someone to brainstorm your attributes and your roles. By using varying combinations, see how others view you—see the universe of you.

7. Another approach utilizing the phrases of this activity is that of self—that is, exploring the universality of mood and feeling. As an individual activity try some of these:

I'm like a warming sun when _____

I'm a shimmering pond when _____

I'm a lengthening shadow when _____

I'm like a winter's chill when _____

I'm a rising tide when _____

I'm like a waning moon when _____

I'm a rainbow when _____

I'm like a song when _____

To utilize the above phrases as a group activity, try having students complete one of the open-ended phrases in an anonymous way—no name. Collect all of the completed statements and read them to the total group. Have all students write on paper the name of the classmate they think completed each statement. Each student keeps a tally sheet on how many classmates correctly associated their names with each statement read.

Afterwards, these questions may be appropriate:

"How many people really know me?"

"In what ways might people really get to know me?"

MORE MIND GLITTER

It would appear that whatever our minds are capable of perceiving there is a storage chamber of things seemingly experienced before. These events may not be clear, but they are there and waiting to be used. It is one of the wonderments of the human mind.

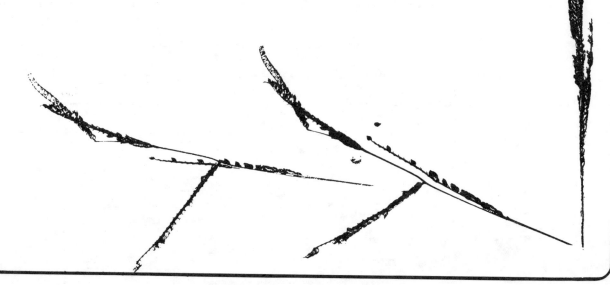

I AM A WORD!

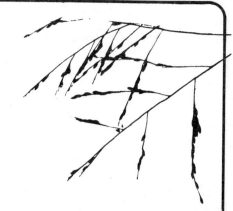

Focus: Humor

Openness

Knowledge

MIND GLITTER

There is a lot to be said for humor. It can turn a frown into a grin and a grin into a smile and a smile into a laugh. It also can remove stress, fear, awkwardness and uneasiness. If you are creating humor, it may reflect originality in your thinking.

PROCEDURES:

Provide a few selected words to a few selected students—words like **odiferous**, **serendipity**, and **reincarnation**.

Tell them to go to the library and look up these words in several dictionaries. Tell them to make sure they gain a full understanding as to their meanings.

DIRECTIONS: Be the word. Imagine you are being pulled out of a bag by your letters. Use body language, hand movements, facial expressions, and sounds to define the word you are. There should be no spoken words during the dramatization. Afterwards, indicate the word you were. Explain why you did certain movements and made certain sounds to define the word's meaning.

EXTENSIONS:

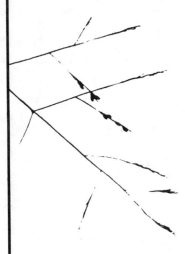

1. Encourage students to search out interesting words in the library to try.

2. Construct a classroom word bag. Encourage students to bring a "new" word to class each week for a dramatiztion. Place the word dramatized in the bag.

3. Encourage application of the words in the word bag. Have students write synonyms of those words in sentences.

4. Provide words from content areas, such as mathematics, science, art, music, and the social sciences for dramatizations.

5. Play games with the words selected such as Charades, Scrabble, etc.

6. If computers and the appropriate software are available, encourage students to create crossword puzzles and word finds with their interesting words.

7. In association with this activity, challenge students to choose the most important 100 words in the English language. Have them imagine that a word bag of 100 words would be shipped to a far distant planet where the inhabitants would use those words in a study of Earth people. Challenge students to develop a criteria by which these words would be chosen.

8. If Socrates suddenly appeared on Earth, what would be the most important ten words to add to his vocabulary. The ten words would be words nonexistent during his lifetime.

**MORE
MIND GLITTER**

How we view the word is a reflection of ourselves.

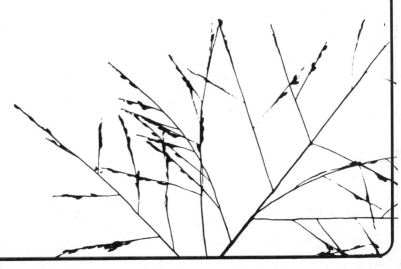

FAIL-SAFE GOAL SETTING

Focus:
Creative Inventiveness
Assessment
Openness

MIND GLITTER

Failure is important to our lives. Some of the most valuable goals come about when we fail. Often from the depths of despair we can see where we want to be. Winning isn't the most important thing. The most important thing is determining what it takes to win, then getting up to try again.

Finding goals when we fail requires assessment, risk taking and fortitude. It takes those attributes to rekindle the human spirit. But in doing so we deal with our own growth and development.

PROCEDURES:
Indicate to students that finding good in bad can be an exercise in creative thinking. What follows are some potential disappointments and failures. The task is to list some possible positive creative effects.

Disappointments/Failures
1. furnace failure
2. sack of rotting apples
3. death of a loved one

4. too much to do and not enough time

Positive Creative Effects
family gathering around a campfire
slow nourishment for plants
attribute listing on things worth remembering
learning how to establish priorities and time management

Disappointments/Failures	Positive Creative Effects
5. loss of a job	_____
6. failing a class or a test	_____
7. teasing	_____
8. being bullied	_____
9. conflict with a parent	_____
10. not enough money	_____
11. unpopularity	_____
12. arguments	_____
13. weight problems	_____
14. lack of confidence	_____
15. loneliness	_____

EXTENSION: Place an ''in what ways can I avoid'' in front of an item chosen from 5-15 and do creative problem solving on that problem.

**MORE
MIND GLITTER**

At a time when failure is felt, try thinking of yourself in terms of a symbol—a symbol that would represent your essence or essential self. You may draw it or construct it. Create something visible, something you can see and touch.

As you see your symbol, remind yourself that since the beginning of time there has never been anyone like you. Never until all life has vanished on this planet will there be another such as you. You are rare. Bring forth this and show the world.

ANALOGY RESEARCH

Focus: Questioning Techniques   Knowledge
             Self-Directed Activity   Resources
             Integration   Assessment
             Humor

MIND GLITTER   *By imagining what it would be like to be something else, we can widen our perspectives. There are many different ways to approach a subject for understanding and enlightenment.*

PROCEDURES: This activity can be a preamble for future research topics. Encourage students to imagine they are the topic they are researching, that within their reports should be their thoughts and feelings.

1. What would it be like to be a leaf that feeds the soil?
2. What would it be like to be a wolf spider?
3. What would it be like to be an ice crystal on a window pane?
4. What would it be like to be a secondary rainbow?
5. What would it be like to be a sand dollar?
6. What would it be like to be a morel mushroom?
7. What would it be like to be an acorn that became an oak tree?
8. What would it be like to be a sunflower?

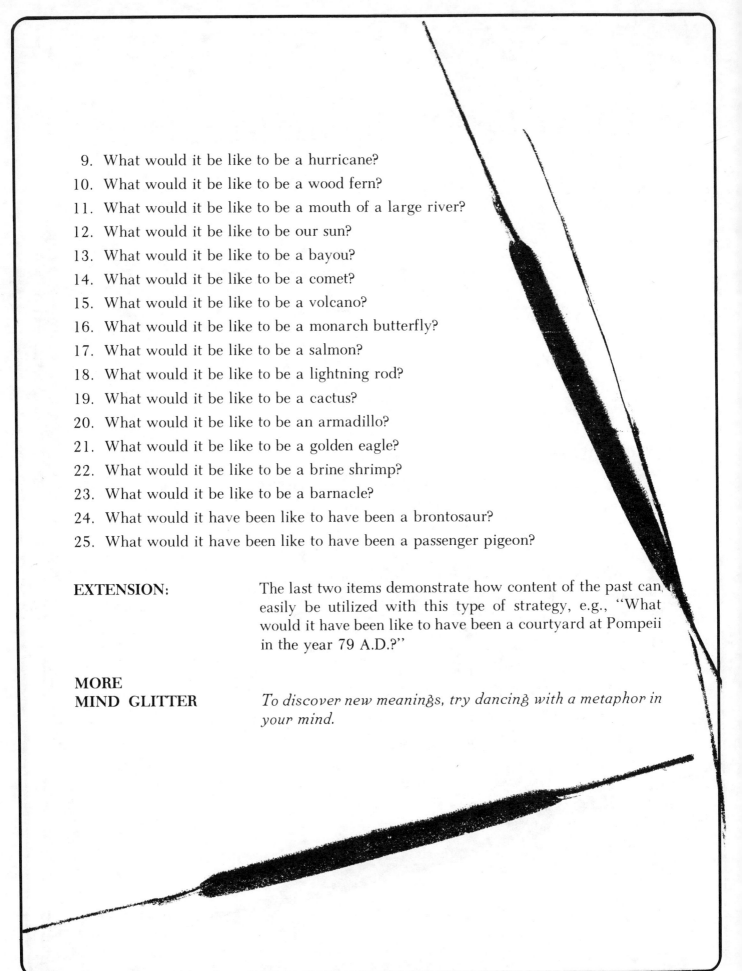

9. What would it be like to be a hurricane?

10. What would it be like to be a wood fern?

11. What would it be like to be a mouth of a large river?

12. What would it be like to be our sun?

13. What would it be like to be a bayou?

14. What would it be like to be a comet?

15. What would it be like to be a volcano?

16. What would it be like to be a monarch butterfly?

17. What would it be like to be a salmon?

18. What would it be like to be a lightning rod?

19. What would it be like to be a cactus?

20. What would it be like to be an armadillo?

21. What would it be like to be a golden eagle?

22. What would it be like to be a brine shrimp?

23. What would it be like to be a barnacle?

24. What would it have been like to have been a brontosaur?

25. What would it have been like to have been a passenger pigeon?

EXTENSION: The last two items demonstrate how content of the past can easily be utilized with this type of strategy, e.g., "What would it have been like to have been a courtyard at Pompeii in the year 79 A.D.?"

MORE MIND GLITTER *To discover new meanings, try dancing with a metaphor in your mind.*

DIFFERENT WAYS OF GIVING A BOOK REPORT

Focus: Creative Inventiveness   Knowledge
              Self-Directed Activity   Resources

MIND GLITTER

Sometimes things begin because they are easy and purposeful. You find others doing them and that gives support to what you are doing. Others see what you are doing and they do it. All of this leads to a norm or par or the expected.

We all need to go back and examine why we do things the way we do them. We need to examine the purposes and the why's.

Variation, I think, is a key word. Continents variate and the rivers on them variate, even the universe variates. We need some variation in our lives: people, teachers and kids. Like a river that finds a better passage way to the sea, there may be better ways of teaching.

PROCEDURES: Next time you think of assigning book reports, try some of these suggestions:

1. Imagine you were a Hollywood screenwriter. What story scenes would you film and what story scenes would you eliminate? Why?

2. Play a record or cassette of a song. Indicate the reasons why your musical choice can be associated with the book you read.

3. Play 20 Questions with your class about the book you read.

4. Draw comic strip frames of the story's plot.

5. Tell how the story would be changed if one of the main characters were eliminated.

6. Create a board game of the story's plot. Tell how the game relates to the story.

7. Write a one-act play about one important chapter in the book.

8. Build three or more "shoe box" settings of the story. Explain the impact of each setting to the story.

9. Do magazine collages of the main characters. Explain each character's relationship to the story.

10. Create a crossword puzzle of the story elements. Explain why you chose the questions you did.

11. Describe all the boring sections of the book.

12. If you could add characters to the story, who would you choose and why?

13. List ten important words in the story. Tell why they're important.

14. Write a one-page summary of the story. Tell what you wanted to add to the page but couldn't.

15. Write a short chapter after the last chapter to redo the book's ending.

16. Write a newspaper-type article about the story plot as though it happened today.

17. Do a "finger puppet" dramatization about one aspect of the story.

18. Assume the role of one of the main characters and tell the story from that character's perspective.

19. List ten important questions on the story. Write ten important answers to the ten important questions.

20. Create a mobile on the story. Utilize parts of the mobile to represent characters, setting, conflict and the resolution of the conflict.

21. Come up with three different story endings from the original.

22. Develop a filmstrip or use overhead projector transparencies to tell the story.

23. Report the story on the basis of likes and dislikes. Have a list of "I like" and a list of "I didn't like . . . ."

24. Create a different and better book cover. Use the inside flap to write a short summary of the story.

25. List five ways you could have improved the story.

26. Add one page to the story that would include you as one of the characters. What did you contribute to the story?

27. List research topics the author probably had to research in order to write the story.

28. Write the essence of the story in poetry.

29. Imagine the story was made into a movie. Write up an ad on it for the newspaper.

30. Do a mock TV broadcast about one or more of the major events in the story.

31. Do a mock interview with the main character of the story. Repeat the answers given with your questions.

32. How might you program a video game utilizing the story elements?

33. Take an object that's important to the story (it could be a house or a car or something else) and write a page or so about being that object. Tell how important you are to the story.

34. Write an imaginary seven-day journal that one of the main characters may have written.

35. Suppose you could interview the book's author. Write five questions you would ask the author and give five responses you would expect the author to answer.

36. Try to tell the book's story in pantomime.

37. Stand up and give a regular book report.

EXTENSIONS:

1. Take a chapter in a textbook and see how many of the mentioned suggestions fit. Try them!

2. Integrate some of the suggestions with an existing curriculum unit. Use the suggestions in learning about specific concepts.

3. Take this activity and, with your students, brainstorm more suggestions. Keep the total listing available in a classroom for encouraging SELF-DIRECTED STUDY.

4. "Different Ways of Giving a Book Report" relates to differentiated and variant talents. By providing options to students you may be cultivating very special talents, talents that may open doors of opportunities for a lifetime. When you ask for a product from students, just open the assignment to many possibilities.

**MORE
MIND GLITTER**

MINDGLOW, to me, means there are new and better ways of doing things.

We do have choices and the choices abound when we look at things from different angles, different perspectives, and different frames of reference.

It is so easy to get into a rut, to get mired in, to have our lights dimmed. Ruts come about through excessive trafficking along a certain path. We all have the qualities from which stars are made. We can be starlike.

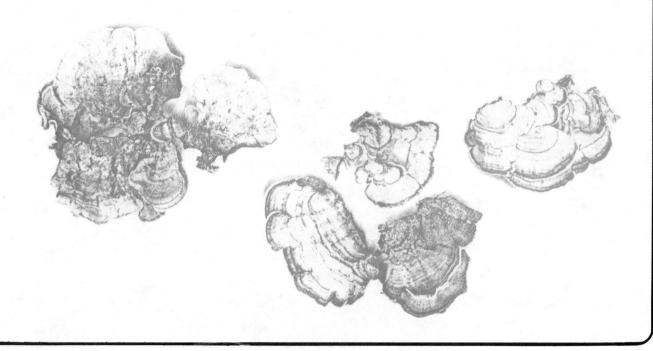

BECOMING

Focus: Questioning Techniques   Knowledge
              Creative Inventiveness   Openness
              Humor   Assessment
              Integration

MIND GLITTER   *Imagining what it would be like to be something else is a play on the paradoxical, the metaphorical, and the analogical of the mind. Within this domain lies many of the higher thought processes.*

PROCEDURES: Take one of these events and either write, dramatize or come up with another way of presenting the experience.

1. Be a green leaf that turns into a bright orange one. Describe how it feels to be marveled at and admired by people who stand below you. Tell about how your color is enjoyed by your animal friends who rest on the branches above you.

2. Be a grape that became a raisin. Describe how it feels to shrink, to shrivel, to become dry and wrinkled.

3. Be a bumper sticker that causes drivers to feel good about themselves. What words do you have that cause smiles and happy feelings? Tell about how you changed a gloomy person into a happy person.

4. Be a cotton ball whose fibers are stretched into strands of thread. Describe how it feels to be reshaped by being pulled apart and stretched into lengthy strands.

5. Be a fireworks rocket on the 4th of July. Tell how you lighted the night sky. Tell about your beautiful pattern and your loud noises. Tell about the ooo's and the ahhh's and the applause you heard.

6. Be an icicle that became air. Describe how it feels to be cold and firm and full of beautiful crystals but only to melt and lose your shape. Describe how it feels as a liquid with the thought of losing your identity to the sun.

7. Be a sunflower. Tell how you greet the sun each morning by turning your neck to the eastern sky. Tell how earthworms tickle your roots during the day. Tell how you bid good night to the sun in the western sky. Tell how it feels to be tall, bright yellow, and happy.

8. Be a candle. Tell how you can make shadows larger on a wall. Tell how you make things comfortable and cozy with your flame. Tell how you cause people to reflect happy memories and to feel good by your glow.

EXTENSION:

In what ways are objects and things like people?

MORE MIND GLITTER

Become a star. All humans are capable of becoming stars. Like a star, we have a center—a center of radiating energies. We are starlike.

We become unstarlike when we dim our lights and withdraw behind dark clouds. We can hurt when we do that because it was not meant to be. We were meant to be stars.

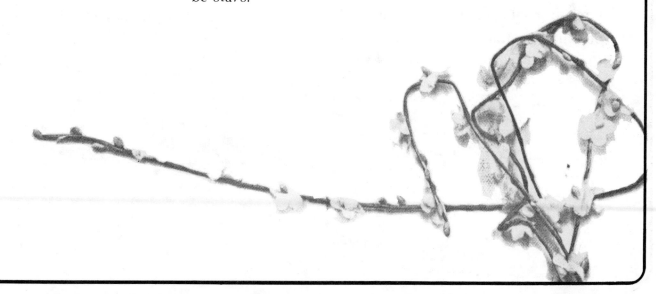

REMEMBRANCES . . .

At one time when I was too young for school, I saw elephants on my front yard. And they were being watered from a fire hydrant. It was on an early morning of summer, and to this day I can recall my feelings. I wanted to run because of fear. I was allured by the sight of something I had never seen before. I stayed with alluring fear! Sometimes I go back to the town I left and to that house. The concrete sidewalk is still broken from a presence of long ago.

The next time I felt alluring fear was a few years after beginning school. During a spring, gypsies came to our house and my mother fed them. My mother is the kindest of all people. I was allured to the wagon of painted colors and to the excitement of the roads they had traveled. And my head danced with the fear of being kidnapped. There were always rumors in those days and I had heard a few.

I sometimes look to the past to analyze the present. My mind is metaphorical and it started long ago. It began with circus elephants and gypsies and the memories of a feeling incurred. The compressed conflict of alluring fear, I discovered much later, is a symbolic analogy. Symbolic analogies are strategies developed by the Synectics Corporation to cause a "poetic stretch" of the imagination. Putting paired antonyms together can do this. Many things of importance in my life have come about by looking at things through symbolic analogies. Whenever I feel alluring fear now, it is an indicator of something important, something I want to investigate.

OPEN-ENDED

Focus: Interpersonal Regard

                    Assessment

MIND GLITTER   *Things that cause us to respond in a simultaneous matter may reflect how we really feel about things. Also, there are many times in our lives where split-second decision making is the only option available.*

PROCEDURES: Utilize statements of this type in a staccato-like fashion. Don't allow too much thinking time and don't ask for volunteers.

Just read the statement and point to a potential respondent.

1. One thing I like about this class is . . .
2. One thing I learned today was . . .
3. A real friend in this class is . . .
4. If I could share something with someone in this class it would be with . . .
5. One person I admire is . . .
6. I feel happiest when . . .
7. Someday I'd like to . . .
8. One person who can make friends easily is . . .
9. I feel best when . . .
10. When I pretend, I pretend that . . .
11. If I had one wish, I'd wish for . . .
12. One person who helps others is . . .
13. I'd like to learn how to . . .
14. One person who cooperates with others is . . .
15. Sometimes I wonder about . . .

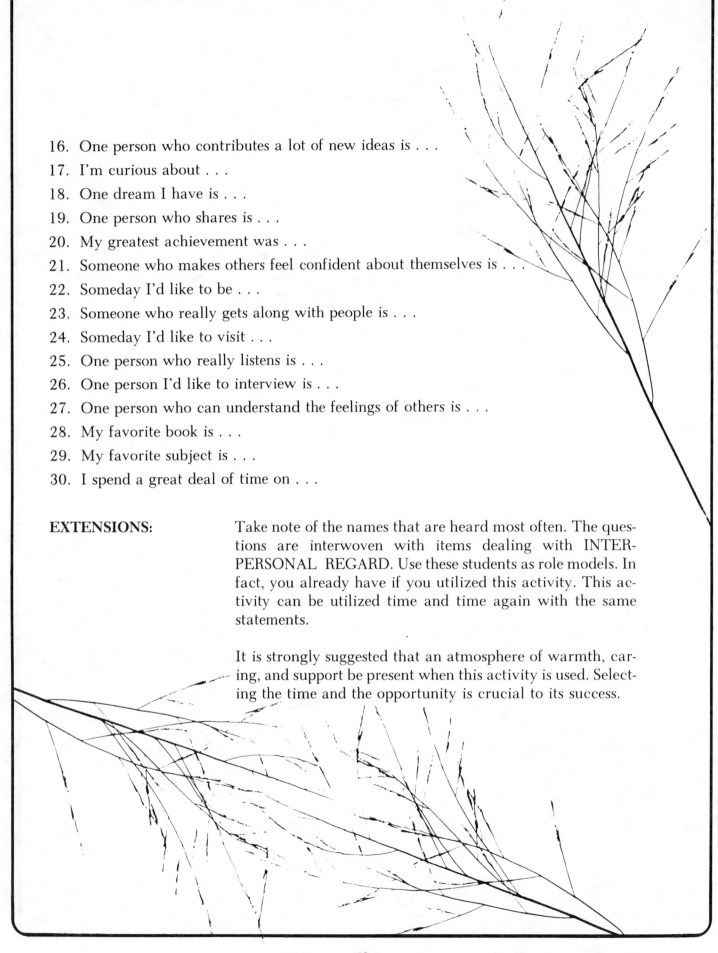

16. One person who contributes a lot of new ideas is . . .
17. I'm curious about . . .
18. One dream I have is . . .
19. One person who shares is . . .
20. My greatest achievement was . . .
21. Someone who makes others feel confident about themselves is . . .
22. Someday I'd like to be . . .
23. Someone who really gets along with people is . . .
24. Someday I'd like to visit . . .
25. One person who really listens is . . .
26. One person I'd like to interview is . . .
27. One person who can understand the feelings of others is . . .
28. My favorite book is . . .
29. My favorite subject is . . .
30. I spend a great deal of time on . . .

EXTENSIONS: Take note of the names that are heard most often. The questions are interwoven with items dealing with INTER-PERSONAL REGARD. Use these students as role models. In fact, you already have if you utilized this activity. This activity can be utilized time and time again with the same statements.

It is strongly suggested that an atmosphere of warmth, caring, and support be present when this activity is used. Selecting the time and the opportunity is crucial to its success.

MIND FOOD

Focus: Questioning Techniques   Openness
Thinking Time   Knowledge
Integration   Assessment

MIND GLITTER   *In every classroom there's a door. And through that door, and perhaps a few other doors, is the most illuminating and rewarding resource room available. It's called the world. Sometimes we take too literally the phrase "a classroom day."*

PROCEDURES: What nutrients are to a plant, analogies are to the mind. With the analogies to follow, there are no correct answers. But do look for and examine the explanations given to support the choices provided. Only use a few of the items at one time.

1. Which provokes more thought?   ____ a window
   Why?   ____ a door

2. Which takes up more space?   ____ a frown
   Why?   ____ a smile

3. Which costs more?   ____ popularity
   Why?   ____ aloneness

4. Which is heavier?　　　　　　　　____ a mountain
   Why?　　　　　　　　　　　　　　 ____ a mistake

5. Which pays a greater dividend?　 ____ an answer
   Why?　　　　　　　　　　　　　　 ____ a question

6. Which is sadder?　　　　　　　　 ____ a gain from someone's loss
   Why?　　　　　　　　　　　　　　 ____ a loss from someone's gain

7. Which is longer?　　　　　　　　 ____ a lie
   Why?　　　　　　　　　　　　　　 ____ a belief

8. Which is taller?　　　　　　　　　____ frustration
   Why?　　　　　　　　　　　　　　 ____ joy

9. Which is more secure?　　　　　　____ a key
   Why?　　　　　　　　　　　　　　 ____ a lock

10. Which is quieter?　　　　　　　　____ moonlight
    Why?　　　　　　　　　　　　　　 ____ embarrassment

11. Which is more exhausting?　　　　____ mountain climbing
    Why?　　　　　　　　　　　　　　 ____ being rejected

12. Which is more comfortable?　　　 ____ a chair
    Why?　　　　　　　　　　　　　　 ____ a diary

13. Which is noisier?   _____ a goal obtained
    Why?   _____ failure

14. Which creates the greatest headache?   _____ achieving
    Why?   _____ underachieving

15. Which is weaker?   _____ a spider's web
    Why?   _____ a promise

EXTENSION: If more are needed throughout the school year, just inter-change words from the items provided. After a while, when students have become accustomed to responding to analogies of this type, try content words like: Which is heavier, a fact or a theory? Which carries more weight, an exclamation point or a question mark?

**MORE
MIND GLITTER**   *Causing analytical minds to explore the potential of metaphorical thought will expand abilities to analyze.*

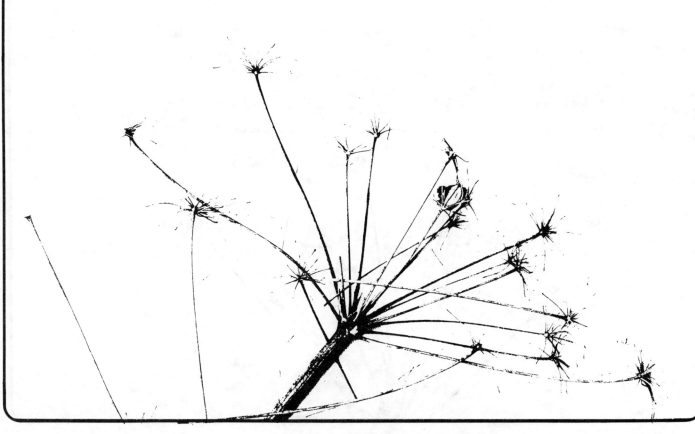

YOU ARE THE WORLD

Focus: Interpersonal Regard
Questioning Techniques

MIND GLITTER *Attributes of everything can be found within you.*

PROCEDURES: Have someone who knows you select and respond to a few of the statements listed below. What they choose should be as interesting as their responses. The only condition is that the responses are not negative.

1. You are like an untraveled path when . . .
2. You are the glowing embers of firewood when . . .
3. You are like a mountain stream when . . .
4. You are like starlight when . . .
5. You are like a mountain when . . .
6. You are like fresh spring rain when . . .
7. You are like the morning fog when . . .
8. You are like a flower when . . .
9. You are like the high tide when . . .
10. You are like the low tide when . . .
11. You are like the silence of a pond when . . .
12. You are like on-rushing water when . . .
13. You are like twilight when . . .
14. You are like a rainbow when . . .
15. You are like thunder when . . .

16. You are like an owl when . . .

17. You are like an eagle when . . .

18. You are like a passing storm when . . .

19. You are like an open field when . . .

20. You are like a gentle wind when . . .

EXTENSIONS:

1. Encourage students to respond to themselves with some chosen selections.

2. Do attribute listing on some selected items. Do human attribute listing on the same items. What kinds of comparisons can be made?

3. In what ways are we the world? In what ways are we the universe?

MORE MIND GLITTER

It's the thing that people do to people. And we've done it—both you and I. If there's hope for the future, they're in your classroom. Help change the thing around to be—doing things for people. Help people see the value in people.

HEARING—SEEING—TOUCHING

Focus: Questioning Techniques
Creative Inventiveness
Integration

MIND GLITTER   *We all don't receive and transmit information in the same way. Some are astute listeners. Some are astute viewers. Some are kinesetic. When we, as teachers, are establishing a way in which students receive information, we need to keep this in mind.*

This exercise will demonstrate this concept.

PROCEDURES: Bring a wire coat hanger to class in order to brainstorm this topic: HOW MANY DIFFERENT USES, FUNCTIONS, OR PURPOSES COULD A CLOTHES HANGER SERVE?

1. Begin the demonstration by simply holding up the hanger and listening to the responses.

2. After a few minutes of student responses, SLOWLY BEGIN TO TWIST THE HANGER into various shapes. In doing this, also change your position of holding it. Give students a different vantage point for viewing the twisted hanger.

3. After several minutes of doing this, give the twisted hanger to a few selected students and encourage them to twist the hanger for additional suggestions as to new and different uses.

You will be amazed about the quantity of ideas generated. The reason, of course, is that you plugged into different ways in which information can be received, dealt with, and applied.

EXTENSIONS:

Consider the following:

1. Make available in your classroom chunks of modeling clay, bell wire, or anything that lends itself to easy modeling or molding. Encourage students to play with ideas while involved with generating ideas. That is, play with ideas in a visual and kinesthetic way.

2. In constructing and implementing curriculum, make provisions for the visual and the kinesthetic.

3. In constructing learning centers, make available things other than just reading materials.

4. When possible while teaching, draw symbols, designs on the chalkboard to reinforce the information you give.

5. Invite human resources into your class to demonstrate the Braille system. Let kids experiment with the system, too. Invite a sculptor to your class to demonstrate how the kinesthetic process is used in molding shapes and figures. Invite a clothes designer to your class to relate how visual thinking is important in creating clothing.

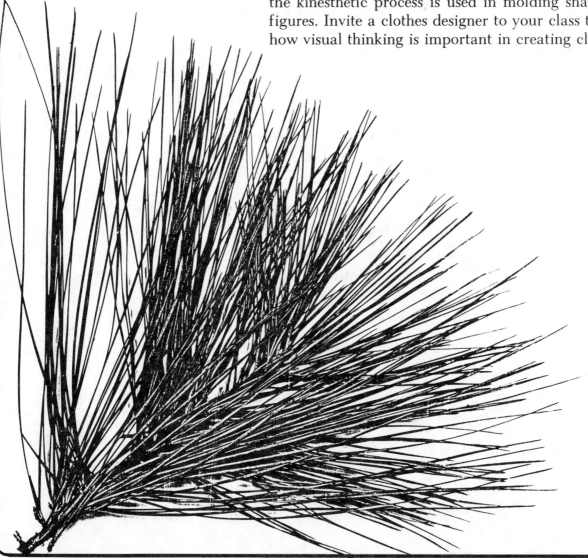

IMPROVING

Focus: Humor
Creative Inventiveness
Integration

MIND GLITTER   *Be it ourselves, an object, or a situation, one of the natural tendencies of the human species is that of improving things. Allowing kids to do this in a classroom is to promote and expand their creative intelligence.*

PROCEDURES: Select an item from the list below and have students draw and label the component parts of their improved or invented item.

1. Improve a bookmark.
2. Come up with a way to wash outside upper story windows from the inside.
3. Design a drinking glass that won't spill.
4. Improve a grocery shopping cart.
5. Improve a desktop.
6. Design a "cleanup" shoe that could be used to pick up crumbs, scraps and other debris from a floor.
7. Improve a wake-up alarm clock.
8. Improve a pocket on a pair of jeans.
9. Come up with a way to get playground balls down from school rooftops
10. Improve a refrigerator.
11. Invent a way to pick up your mail without opening a door.
12. Improve a drinking fountain to avoid getting sprayed in the face.
13. Come up with a dinner utensil for eating spaghetti.
14. Improve a school lunch box.
15. Invent a pair of sure-hold tongs.

EXTENSIONS:
As a total class, think of ways to improve the following:

1. taking attendance and lunch count
2. dealing with boredom in a cafeteria lunch line
3. study habits
4. learning centers
5. utilizing community resources
6. planning a field trip
7. parent conferences
8. classroom organization
9. assessing student progress
10. the school grounds

**MORE
MIND GLITTER**

By being involved in the improvement of things, the transfer of improving self is likely. It may not come quickly, but the process has been seeded in the mind.

I'm trying to improve myself by becoming quieter and stronger. I've discovered that it takes real strength to become quieter.

When I'm with classroom kids, we start the day with five minutes of quietness. And then, we share our thoughts. With a lot of kids it takes strength to share their thoughts. Quietness, strength and gaining a perspective on things are good ways of starting a day. It makes a good foundation for improving things, especially the improvement of self.

EMEMBRANCES

One time in the Appalachian Mountains of North Carolina, I jumped fully clothed into a creek. I was involved in teaching in a summer program for gifted and talented kids. The kids I taught had just completed their junior year in high school prior to enrolling there. They were really neat kids, and they liked what we did. One hot, sweltering day after school, they asked me if I would jump into a creek with them.

Several of them asked of me a lot of other things. They wanted to know how I related to them as individuals. They wanted to know how I related to life and how I saw them in relationship to life. These questions were extremely important to them at that time and place in their lives. Our school days were full, and my evenings that were once free, suddenly became full. I still remember those kids and, I think, they still remember me.

Mentoring today is an important concept especially in gifted and talented education. Mentor was Odysseus' **trusted** counselor, under whose disguise Athena became the guardian and teacher of Telemachus. I mention this because there are some educational programs that are assigning "mentors" to individual kids. Ruth Noller wrote a book entitled **Mentoring: A Voiced Scarf** (Noller, 1982). Her title reflects to a great degree what mentoring is. It is also a **trusting** relationship that involves two or more people jumping fully clothed into the same creek.

JUDGING

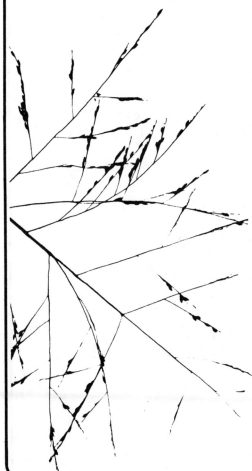

Focus: Openness
Assessment

MIND GLITTER

I want to judge ideas, processes and products. I don't want to judge people. I want to accept people. I can judge ideas, processes and products through a criteria. My criteria might include my values, but that's o.k. It's o.k. because I'm me and I value my values.

PROCEDURES:

Begin this exercise by having students imagine there is a problem in the selection and purchase of a bicycle. Indicate that one way to deal with this problem is to establish a criteria by which a selection can be made.

A criteria might include items such as cost, durability, comfort, appearance, speed and braking power. Measuring the choices available through a criteria is the best way of choosing a solution to my problem.

This exercise deals with criterion building. It begins with rather simple judgements and progresses to some rather difficult ones.

List as many judgements as you can through brainstorming.

1. How do you judge pizza?
2. How do you judge a book?
3. How do you judge a stereo?
4. How do you judge a school day?
5. How do you judge a job?
6. How do you judge leadership?
7. How do you judge a friendship?
8. How do you judge happiness?
9. How do you judge success?
10. How do you judge justice?

EXTENSIONS:

After the brainstorming of criteria items, then consider these options:

1. Use this appraisal system, step-by-step, in selecting the five best criteria items.

   . . . Which criteria items can we modify or combine?

   . . . Which criteria items reflect our concerns and priorities?

   . . . Which criteria items are the most important?

2. Group consensus:
   Give each member of your class five votes to select the criteria items brainstormed. The election determines the choices.

3. Numerical ratings:
   Give each criteria item brainstormed a numerical rating based on the following point values:
   1 point for slight importance
   2 points for average importance
   3 points for high importance

   The five criteria items with the highest scores would represent the criteria.

4. For a complete overview of solution-finding and the creative problem-solving process refer to **Creative Problem-Solving: The Basic Course** (Isaksen and Treffinger, 1985).

MORE MIND GLITTER

Consider this:

What goes into your judgement of a day?
What goes into your judgement of a sunset?
What goes into your judgement of beauty?
What goes into your judgement of ugliness?

I'm much more interested in the above than the judgements made on children in a faculty lounge!

ANSWERS AND QUESTIONS

Focus: Questioning Techniques   Thinking Time
Interpersonal Regard   Integration

MIND GLITTER

It is important to have some base from which we depart, be it the comfort of home and friends or to launch expanding waves of thought.

By viewing an answer as a home base, we can focus on universal issues and how we relate to them.

PROCEDURES:

Try providing an answer and have students develop questions. Encourage students to extend their thinking so that many questions are generated.

Example: The answer is **COMMUNICATION**!

List some questions!

1.   What is the function of language?
2.   What is sending and receiving?
3.   What is an important aspect of marriage and family?
4.   What helps families function together as a unit?
5.   What is an important element of friendship?
6.   How might world peace come about?
7.   How are ideas and feelings transmitted?
8.   What is the purpose of creative expression?
9.   How might human misunderstandings be resolved?

EXTENSIONS:

1. Expand academic concepts by using this approach.

   Examples: The answer is pyramid! What are some questions? This answer is, for every action there's an opposite and equal reaction! What are some questions?

2. Help students realize what their values are by using this approach.

3. Focus on your teaching philosophy by saying: The answer is teaching. What are the questions? Then try: The answer is learning! What are the questions? Then determine which questions are compatible and not compatible.

4. Try this approach before beginning a unit of study. See how many questions will be dealt with. If the questions are not dealt with, ask yourself "why?"

5. Try administering a test based on answers for the purposes of writing questions.

6. Try providing students with a paradoxical or ambiguous situation. Follow the paradox with an answer; then ask for questions. Look for inductive reasoning with your students' responses.

7. If you are familiar with the steps of creative problem solving, use this approach with the "mess-finding" stage of the process.

8. Interview a student by having him respond to an answer by asking questions. This approach can clarify thinking on a number of issues. Another approach is to say, "The answer is Jane Doe? What are the questions?" Allow Jane Doe to structure those questions for herself.

MORE MIND GLITTER

There are different kinds of vision. To lose sight of aspirations, dreams, and goals may be the greatest loss of vision imaginable.

STARSUN OR SUNSTAR?

Focus: Self-Directed Activity
Resources
Integration

MIND GLITTER

Expanding on an idea causes one to look at things in different ways. When different frames of reference are used in problem solving, choices abound in astonishing numbers.

PROCEDURES:

Divide your class into two teams. Have one team brainstorm how many stars there are. Have the other team brainstorm how many suns there are.

Brainstorming Problem:

The sun is a star. A star is a sun. Are there more stars than suns or more suns than stars?

Rules:

1. After ten minutes of brainstorming, each team may use dictionaries, encyclopedias, phone books and other resources.

2. The team brainstorming stars may use only one named star from such categories as entertainment, sports, comics, etc. Both teams may use as many constellations as they can find.

3. The first team that can generate either 100 suns or stars is the winner!

Some Examples:

Suns: The **Baltimore Sun** newspaper, sunflower, Sunday, North Star.

Stars: Helmet design of the Dallas Cowboys, Earth's sun, Michael Jackson, Star Ship *Enterprise*.

EXTENSIONS:

Try a similar approach with:
. . . roads and streets
. . . houses and homes
. . . rocks and stones

Try combinations like:
. . . bats and balls
. . . sticks and stones
. . . hills and valleys

**MORE
MIND GLITTER**

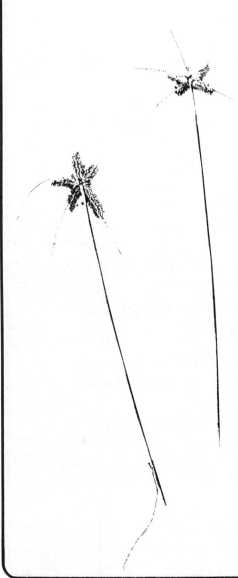

We live in different environments. Sometimes a certain environment can generate complacency or satisfaction and the creative energies diminish.

I believe one way to extend creative potential is by nourishing metaphorical thinking. By looking at relationships among things, we can move into different environments—environments that generate new waves of creative energy within us.

Another way of changing environments for creative expansion is that of "role casting." In your classroom try assigning certain roles to students as they pursue a topic. For example, in this activity some roles might include:

. . . gathering information like a newspaper reporter.
. . . gathering information like an astronomer.
. . . gathering information like a sports historian.
. . . gathering information like a librarian.
. . . gathering information like a geographer.
. . . gathering information like a botanist.
. . . gathering information like a telephone operator would in receiving "information" calls.

INTERPERSONALIZING REGARD FOR OTHERS

Focus: Interpersonal Regard

Assessment

MIND GLITTER

There is a balance in nature—an order of beautiful significance. Sometimes things get out of balance, and we as people have made it so.

Having a balance, an order of things in a classroom, is important. The key element, it would appear, is that of having INTERPERSONAL REGARD towards others.

PROCEDURES:

Utilize this activity early in the year as a means for GOAL SETTING those aspects of INTERPERSONAL REGARD in your classroom.

Provide the scales to your students and have them mark with an "o" where they are now. Have them mark with an "x" where they would like to be.

Maintain the student scales in folders so that periodic reviews can be made. Schedule conferences with individual students for progress reports.

	No	Sometimes	Yes
DO I ACCEPT HELP FROM OTHERS?			
DO I COOPERATE WITH OTHERS?			
DO I FOLLOW RULES?			
DO I GET ALONG WITH OTHERS?			
DO I GET OTHERS TO COOPERATE?			

	No	Sometimes	Yes
DO I GIVE ADVICE WITHOUT BEING RESENTED?			
DO I GIVE NEW IDEAS IN A DISCUSSION?			
DO I HELP OTHER PEOPLE?			
DO I LEAD A DISCUSSION?			
DO I LISTEN TO OTHERS?			
DO I MAKE FRIENDS EASILY?			
DO I MAKE OTHERS FEEL CONFIDENT?			
DO I ORGANIZE PEOPLE?			
DO I PERSUADE OTHERS?			
DO I SHARE BLAME WITH OTHERS?			
DO I SHARE CREDIT WITH OTHERS?			
DO I SHARE THINGS?			
DO I TAKE TURNS?			
DO I UNDERSTAND THE FEELINGS OF OTHERS?			

EXTENSIONS:

In working with individual students on specific items for improvement, use the "IWWMI" method with a divergent/convergent pattern.

"IWWMI" means "In what ways might I?"

Example: "In what ways might I accept help from others?"

After a number of responses have been given (divergent thinking), ask:

"Which of these ways would you feel most comfortable about doing (convergent thinking)?"

MORE MIND GLITTER

I share important things with the students I teach. I share how I feel about things. My students are important to me and that is why I share.

If I succeed, then my students will give something of themselves to the world. And that will become important to them.

REMEMBRANCES

When my daughter Lindley was about due to see the world, I was teaching a sixth grade class. I was really a nervous, expectant father. Well, I got a phone call at school. I told my class what the situation was and I just left. This scenario occurred in the morning and by late afternoon, in the waiting room, it dawned on me I forgot to make arrangements with the school office for a substitute teacher.

Fearing a letter in my file or loss of pay, or loss of job, I meekly entered school the next morning. The music teacher was the first to see me, and she remarked how well my class behaved in the music room yesterday. I received a similar compliment from the physical education teacher; too. Now, I was really beginning to wonder. Every class I ever taught had a reputation for noise and enthusiasm, and it usually spilled over into their other classes.

By this time I could hardly wait until my class assembled. They all came in with smiles on their faces and wanted to know if I was a new father. I said, "It was a false alarm, but what I wanted to know was what happened yesterday?" One kid said, "Well we sort of figured you had some things on your mind, so we just took your lesson plans and did them. No one really knew you were gone except us!"

SELF-DIRECTED ACTIVITY is cited throughout this book as something that is important in a classroom—something to nurture among students. It is a difficult one to nurture, but it has something to do with caring and trusting and developing a positive relationship with those you teach.

EXPERIENCING

Focus: Creative Inventiveness   Knowledge

              Self-Directed Activity   Openness

              Thinking Time   Resources

MIND GLITTER

Information can be found in other places than just textbooks, encyclopedias, and libraries. The best experiences are direct experiences—seeing the potential of the metaphor, discovering through inquiry and learning from the paradoxical.

We should involve students in gathering information from the world around them.

PROCEDURES:

Provide these kinds of choices to your students:

1. Make a report on the structure of spiderwebs. Do not use photographs, books, or other people as resources.

2. Learn all you can about an ant society without reading about ants.

3. Try to choreograph a dance based on the feeding habits of sea gulls.

4. Observe the imperfections and perfections of different leaves within a given species. Then tell how each leaf that ever was is different from any other leaf.

5. Train brine shrimp to do something.

6. Capture and observe a moth for three days. Report on your findings.

7. Construct a hand-held model car that can go forwards and backwards using only the power generated from a mousetrap.

8. Invent a spaghetti fork that improves the eating of spaghetti.

9. Invent a strong adhesive or glue from materials found only in your kitchen. How many pounds can it hold if attached to a wall?

10. Create an electrical alarm system using only paper clips, a flashlight battery, a bulb, paper and masking tape.

EXTENSIONS:

1. Look at the structure of things like
   . . . a hornet's nest
   . . . a dandelion spore
   . . . a wildflower

   In what ways are they like
   . . . a home?
   . . . a community?
   . . . a nation?

2. Take one of the topics in any of the ten sentences and brainstorm the "IWWMI." In other words, **In What Ways Might I** gain information on this topic?

3. If you are familar with the processes of creative problem solving, utilize one of the 1-10 items as the "mess!" Do creative problem solving in developing a problem statement, a solution, and the implementation of that solution.

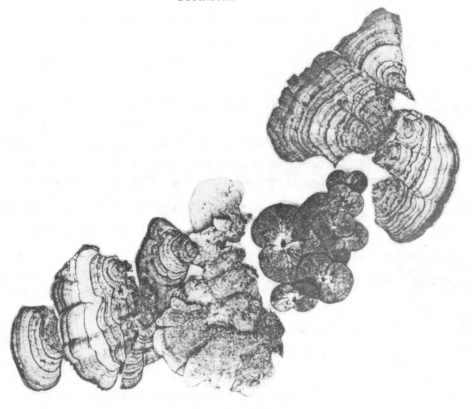

SEASHELLS OR HOW TO ORGANIZE A TOPIC FOR CREATIVE EXPRESSION

Focus: Resources   Humor

Knowledge   Self-Directed Activity

MIND GLITTER   *Because there are differences in a classroom—different learning styles, different kinds of hemispheric dominances, different kinds of intellectual talents and different ways of knowing—a teacher should open alternative paths to knowledge.*

There are many, many modes of creative expression that are ideal for expressing what we've learned and what we know.

PROCEDURES: Indicate to students there are different ways of expanding a topic and different ways of expressing what you know about it. As an example, take the topic of seashells! Listen to these choices; select one and do it!

1.   Create a mime production of a seashell being washed in by the sea.
2.   Create a cartoon strip featuring three different kinds of seashells.
3.   Determine a kind of seashell that could serve different functions. How many different functions could it serve?
4.   Write a story about a lonely seashell that became famous.
5.   Write a biography of a seashell.
6.   Create your own seashell.

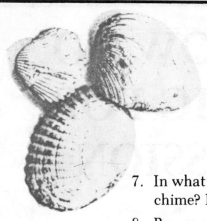

7. In what ways could you construct a seashell mobile or wind chime? Do it!

8. Become a seashell and tell about your life.

9. Write a poem about a seashell.

10. In what ways could seashells serve society?

11. Compile some seashell jokes.

12. Do some "mad libs" about seashells.

13. What are the attributes of a seashell?

14. Construct an unusual centerpiece using seashells.

15. Build a musical instrument using seashells.

16. Compare and contrast seashells. What shells would you classify as "superheroes" and why?

17. Draw the inside of a seashell as seen by a snail.

18. Use seashell designs to create a batik.

19. Do a personality or character sketch of a seashell.

20. Create some original seashell jewelry.

21. Think of ways to preserve a delicate seashell. Do it!

22. Use glue and seashells to build a futuristic space station.

23. In what ways could a modified seashell design serve society?

24. What kinds of world changes would occur if there were no seashells?

25. Describe ways in which you are like a seashell.

EXTENSIONS:

1. Encourage students to read Anne Morrow Lindbergh's book, **Gift from the Sea**—a book of beauty and wisdom.

   Read excerpts of this book to your students. Share the reasons why you chose the selections you read.

2. Have students add to the list of topics.

3. Extend thinking into metaphorical realms by asking questions like . . .

   In what ways is a seashell like giving and receiving?

   In what ways is a seashell like "forever"?

   In what ways is a seashell like a woman? a man? a child?

   In what ways is a seashell like a galaxy?

   In what ways is a seashell like infinity?

4. Determine how many students chose construction, chose drama, chose research, chose writing, chose drawing, chose thought questions, etc. Encourage the use of these talents as a means of expressing self.

5. Select a day and call it Seashell Day. Display student creations and provide time for presentations on this day.

MORE MIND GLITTER

The things of real beauty—the things that can elevate one's mind from the stress and the argumentation of life need not be purchased—they're here and have been for millions of years. Go to the seashore or a mountaintop and receive. Or find them in your mind; they're there, too!

REMEMBRANCES

A friend of mine used to nudge me a lot in the ribs. The nudges were always followed with challenges about how was I going to accommodate different kinds of intellectual talent in a classroom. I knew at the time, as everyone in the universe knew, that I.Q. and achievement tests could not measure more than what they measured, and that was very little.

After a while, my rib cage was really beginning to hurt. And I really began to think. Now I had this cute little girl in my classroom who never raised her hand and didn't participate much in class discussions. I had an intuitive feeling this girl really had some talent, but I had no idea what it was. In association with my ribs, I sat down with an art teacher, a music teacher, and a physical education teacher and we talked about talents. We talked about visualization and rhythm and movement and a lot of talents I wasn't reaching in my classroom. The little girl in my classroom began to raise her hand and contribute to class discussions in a very meaningful way.

Well, time causes change. The guy who nudged me a lot in the ribs wrote **Scamper** and some other books. I went through a couple of moves, a couple of jobs and wrote a few books. And one night while watching **Saturday Night Live** on television, I saw my little girl. I saw her the next Saturday and many Saturdays after that. Thanks, Bob, for the painful nudges, and thanks to you, Lauri, for making it happen.

CROSSOVER

Focus: Questioning Techniques   Thinking Time
Integration

MIND GLITTER

Expanding thought processes is what education should be about. Creating paradoxes can do this because they deal with the "what if's" and the "what might happen's." They deal with the transplantations imagined and this is important, because in all of our lives we will deal with the transplantations that are real—the ones that will require of us the skills of problem solving.

PROCEDURES:

Select an item from the list below for occasional usage. They require thinking time, so provide for the contemplation required.

1. What is the sound of a rainbow?
2. What is the taste of happiness?
3. What is the texture of sadness?
4. What is the structure of comfort?
5. What is the sound of a shadow?
6. What is the taste of a promise?
7. What is the texture of memories?
8. What is the sculpture of loneliness?
9. What is the musical chord of a mistake?
10. What is the taste of candlelight?
11. What is the fabric of wishes?
12. What is the color of caring?
13. What is the sound of infinity?
14. What is the flavor of laughter?
15. What is the texture of fear?
16. What is the weight of commitment?
17. What is the sound of silence?
18. What is the taste of twilight?
19. What is the apparel of fog?
20. What is the vision of warmth?
21. What is the sound of winter snow?
22. What is the cost of an emotion?
23. What is the size of knowing?

EXTENSION:

Try building a single response into a statement and then look at the meaning suggested.

Example: I hear rainbows because I dream.

MINDWRITING[1]

Focus:
Creative Inventiveness   Integration
Interpersonal Regard   Openness
Thinking Time   Assessment

MIND GLITTER

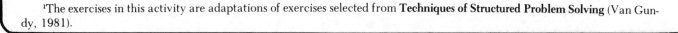

So many of earth's people are visual thinkers. The visual imprint of a word, a symbol or an image can stimulate associations and experiences that lead to new possibilities. As teachers or as people dealing with people, it is important to note what avenues are best for giving and receiving information. Misinformation and misinterpretation can be dragons to our lives.

PROCEDURES:

MINDWRITING is the same as brainwriting. Brainwriting is a term that originated from the Battelle Institute research unit on innovation and creativity in Frankfurt, Germany. Arthur B. Van Gundy in his book, **Techniques of Structured Problem Solving** (Van Nostrand Reinhold, 1981), does an excellent review of exercises designed to develop both individual and group ideational processes.

At times in group brainstorming, there may be an individual or two that attempts to dominate the session. This can lead to a threatening situation for other participants. This type of a situation can limit idea production. Although the judging of ideas during a brainstorming session is discouraged, it can happen. MINDWRITING can eliminate the above-mentioned concerns.

[1]The exercises in this activity are adaptations of exercises selected from **Techniques of Structured Problem Solving** (Van Gundy, 1981).

In doing MINDWRITING with a small group, try having everyone:

1. Silently write down one idea to a problem on an index card.

2. Pass the card to the person on the right.

3. Upon receipt of the card do **one** of several options:

    A. Use the idea received to stimulate another idea and write it on the card.

    B. **Modify** the idea and write this modification on the card.

    C. Write a completely new idea on the card.

Within a few minutes many ideas will be generated. It is suggested that the rotation of cards continues until several cards have been totally written on or completed. Upon completion, organize the ideas into categories and tape them to a wall or pin them to a bulletin board. Select the best ideas from each category through a predetermined criteria. Criteria items might include but are not limited to some of the following:

> costs, time, effect on objective, resources, effect on people, easy to do, fits the situation, understood by others, motivation, low hostility, socially acceptable, generates positiveness, generally acceptable, safety, durable, etc.

A criteria of four to five items would be effective in selecting the most promising ideas. The use of a grid is advised.

List criteria items here ↓

Write ideas here ↘

Total point values here ↘

Assign 3 points to a great idea.
Assign 2 points to a workable idea.
Assign 1 point to a maybe workable idea.

Note: One reason for categorizing ideas on a wall or a bulletin board is to create a visual display from which ideas can be easily combined. It also has a tendency to broaden possible solutions to the problem on the evaluative criteria grid.

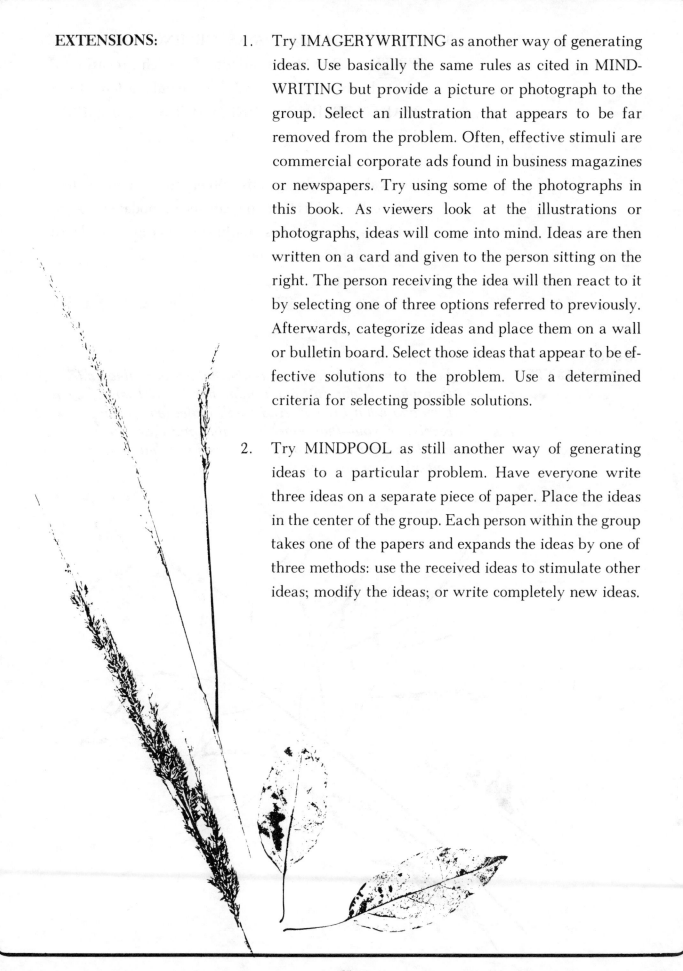

EXTENSIONS:

1. Try IMAGERYWRITING as another way of generating ideas. Use basically the same rules as cited in MIND-WRITING but provide a picture or photograph to the group. Select an illustration that appears to be far removed from the problem. Often, effective stimuli are commercial corporate ads found in business magazines or newspapers. Try using some of the photographs in this book. As viewers look at the illustrations or photographs, ideas will come into mind. Ideas are then written on a card and given to the person sitting on the right. The person receiving the idea will then react to it by selecting one of three options referred to previously. Afterwards, categorize ideas and place them on a wall or bulletin board. Select those ideas that appear to be effective solutions to the problem. Use a determined criteria for selecting possible solutions.

2. Try MINDPOOL as still another way of generating ideas to a particular problem. Have everyone write three ideas on a separate piece of paper. Place the ideas in the center of the group. Each person within the group takes one of the papers and expands the ideas by one of three methods: use the received ideas to stimulate other ideas; modify the ideas; or write completely new ideas.

3. Try a blend of BRAINSTORMING and MINDWRITING. Provide ten minutes for each process on a selected problem. Try varying combinations from BRAINSTORMING, MINDWRITING, IMAGERY-WRITING, and MINDPOOL.

The value in doing this, other than those values previously cited, is that you can accommodate those individuals who learn best auditorily and those who learn best through visualization.

**MORE
MIND GLITTER**

Judge from what I give you—that which is usable and that which is not. But don't judge me on the basis of what I am and what I'm not. And I will judge from what I receive of you—that which is usable and that which is not. I will not judge you on the basis of what you are and what you are not.

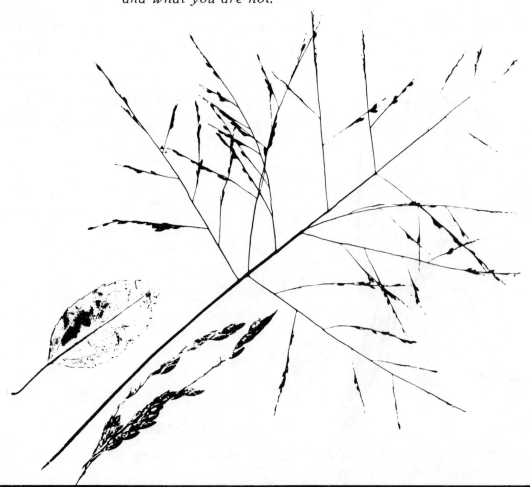

SUPPOSE

Focus:

Questioning Techniques   Thinking Time

Self-Directed Activity   Resources

Interpersonal Regard   Assessment

Openness   Knowledge

MIND GLITTER

How we view the world is a reflection of ourselves.

PROCEDURES:

Occasionally use one of these challenges and provide a day or so of thinking time:

1. Suppose Jules Verne was alive today. What might be three of his latest book titles?

2. Suppose you could bring something back that is extinct. What would it be and why?

3. Suppose you could interview someone from the past. Who would you interview and why?

4. Suppose there was a three-year drought in the Midwest. In what specific ways would your life be affected?

5. Suppose the letter **e** was eliminated from our language. What would be the most important word losses and why?

6. Suppose you had to define **happiness**. What four specific criteria items would you use to measure it?

7. Suppose the year is 1900. What things would be eliminated from your life on a weekend? What things would be added to your life on a weekend?

8. Suppose you could change one historical event from the past. What would you change and why? What would be the effect of this change?

9. Suppose there was a communication blackout for one month in this country. What would be some specific effects? Begin thinking in these terms: What would happen to your assets if they were invested? What would happen to sports attendance figures?

10. Suppose one of your wishes could come true. What would it be and why did you wish it?

EXTENSIONS:

1. Provide some library resource time and challenge students to come back to class with a SUPPOSE question.

2. Encourage students to ask their families and adult friends to come up with an important SUPPOSE question.

3. In what ways would a SUPPOSE question reflect values and beliefs?

4. What tells us more about a person—the answers they give to a question or the questions they ask for an answer?

MORE MIND GLITTER

Anything of beauty has significance. Anything of significance has beauty.

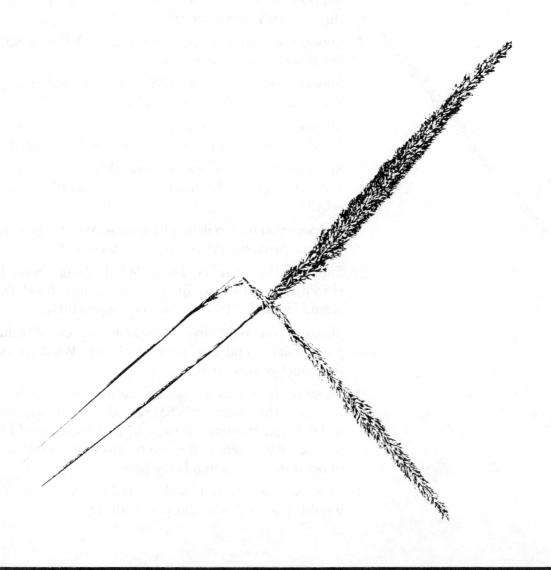

AN IMAGINARY VOYAGE

Focus: Creative Inventiveness

Self-Directed Activity

Knowledge

Integration

MIND GLITTER

The big perspective is that life is a staircase. Knowing what step you are on today is helpful for tomorrow's foothold on the next rung.
For every goal there should be subgoals and for every subgoal there should be a plan of action. Just take one step at a time and sometimes, when the time is right, it is possible to take a giant stride.

PROCEDURES:

Imaginative imagery can tap the resources of both hemispheres of the human brain. Try this simple exercise and observe the results.

Just read the script slowly with long pauses between sentences.

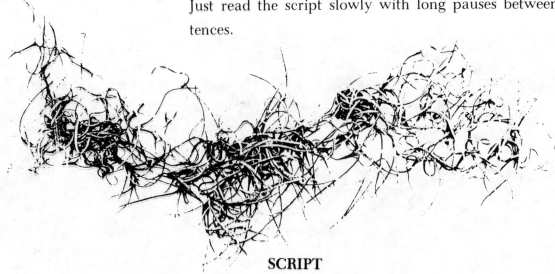

SCRIPT

Close your eyes and relax.

Imagine you are in a land of emerald green foliage.

There is an interplay of light and shadow.

And there is a path and you follow that path.

As you travel the path, the interplay of light on shadow diminishes, and you walk in darkness.

You feel the softness of foliage against your face and you feel reassured.

You are no longer afraid.

You feel that you are on the verge of a great discovery, and your pace quickens.

You see the interplay of light and shadow once again, and the light commands the darkness.

You come to the end of the path, and before you are steps of broken grey stone.

You climb the steps carefully until you see the last step.

And you pause.

Tell students to open their eyes!

Share the photograph in this activity and say, "Does this picture symbolize what you imagined? If not, make it fit into your fantasy. You are this close to an important discovery."

Have students resume the fantasy with closed eyes. Have them reach the top of the steps to find their discovery.

EXTENSIONS:

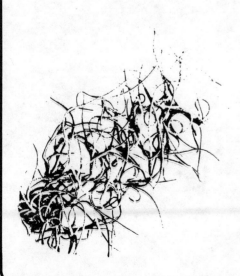

1. Encourage students to write about their discoveries. If they want, they may draw images or symbols of what they discovered.

   Note: Students will probably demonstrate a vastly improved style of writing and storytelling.

2. To make further application of imagery and this exercise, try having students take aspects of their discovery at the top of the stone steps and apply them as potential solutions to a specific problem.

3. Try this approach with a variety of scripts. Try having students assume the character of a fictional or factual individual in a book and how they would react to an imaginary excursion. The results can prove very interesting.

4. There are many varied applications of imagery in problem solving and creative expression. See **Imagery and Creative Imagination** (Khatena, 1984).

CELEBRATE!

*Let your mind glow with the uniqueness
that is yours,*

*Let it sing a song never heard before
or ever again,*

*For nothing like you has ever been before
or ever again.*

REJOICE!

Bob Stanish